Knights of the Golden Circle Treasure Signs

By

Dr. Roy William Roush, Ph.D

Published by Front Line Press

Copyright July 2006

ISBN: 0-9723072-4-9

Proudly Printed in the United States of America

Copies of this book can be ordered from Front Line Press

5150 Escobedo, Woodland Hills, CA 91364

or from the Website, Knightsofthegoldencircle.net

Cover: Photos of some of the carefully shaped rocks made by members of the Knights of the Golden Circle that were placed as markers around their treasure sites.

All rights reserved. No part of this book may be used, reproduced, photocopied, stored in any retrieval system, recorded, or transmitted by any means whatsoever without written permission from the author or publisher (except for brief quotes, reviews, references, or excerpts provided proper credit is given.)

DEDICATION

I dedicate this book to my fellow treasure hunters everywhere--to those of us who will forever be young at heart and in spirit, for we will always follow that big rainbow in the sky for the promise of gold and fortune at its end—and to be sure, my friends, much of it is still out there just waiting to be found.

Also, to two of my old treasure hunting partners who are no longer with us, Colonel Gordon "Gordo" Cooper, one of the Original Seven "Right Stuff" Mercury Astronauts who set many unbroken world records in space, and was the best fighter pilot I ever flew with--and to Steve Ryland, owner of Cal-Gold and Pro-Mack-South treasure and gold prospecting shops.

And to my brother, Donald, in Dallas who is also a treasure hunter, and to my wife, Lydia, for her patience during the writing of this book.

Other Credits of Dr. Roy William Roush

Author of a prize-winning book: *Open Fire*, a major 707-page story of personal, front line combat experience with the 2nd Marine Division during the epic battles of Guadalcanal, Tarawa, Saipan and Tinian in the South Pacific during World War II against the Japanese. The book was awarded the "Best Non-fiction Book of 2004" by the Book Publicists of Southern California.

Author is also featured in the best selling video game by Electronic Arts Entertainments (EA) *Medal of Honor--The Rising Sun*, and *The Assault on Tarawa describing the combat scenes.*

Also author of: *The Mysterious and Secret Order of the Knights of the Golden Circle; How To Find The Treasures of the Knights of the Golden Circle; Lost Treasure Secrets;* and *Fugitives from Freedom.*

Columnist, feature story writer and staff member of: *Treasure; Treasure Search; Treasure Found; Treasure Diver; Treasure Hunter; Treasure News;* and *The CB Guide Magazine.*

Co-editor and feature writer: *Treasure Hunter Confidential Newsletter.*

Contributing editor: *Biblical and American Archeologist Newsletter.*

Editor: *Adventures' Club News of Los Angeles.*

Columnist and reporter: *The Kansas City Star; Rocky Mountain Aviation Magazine; Fabulous Las Vegas Magazine; Stillwater News Press;* and the *O'Collegian.*

Technical writer for Aerospace Companies for 27 years.

Professor: UCLA and Los Angeles City Colleges.

Featured in: *The Treasure of Elysian Park* on the Television Series *"Unsolved Mysteries"* --Also on John Burrud's *Treasure Series* --On NBC's *Special on Diving For Spanish Treasure Galleons in Varacruz, Mexico* --On ABC's Series on *How to Find Lost Treasures* and *The Hunt for Amazing Treasures* --The Frank Sayer Show on *The Lost Dutchman Mine* --and *American Treasure Hunters in Search of 17 Tons of Gold*, filmed by the Tokyo Broadcasting --Plus numerous other radio and television newscasts.

Also as consultant on the upcoming TV documentary *The Loot of Lima*, plus consultant on the soon to be released *National Treasure II, Book of Secrets* by Walt Disney/Jerry Bruckheimer Studio.

BA, Journalism and Ph.D in Biblical Archaeology.

Foreword 1

Chapter One
Who Were the Knights Of The Golden Circle? 3
- *Many thousands were members* 3
- *Plans to restart The Civil War* 4
- *Hiding of Treasures* 4
- *Did The KGC Find Old Spanish Treasure* 4
- *Jesse and Frank James* 5

Chapter Two
KGC Treasure Signs and Symbols
- *Three of Their Treasure Sites* 7
  - New Mexico 7
  - Arkansas 7
  - Kansas 7
  - Favored Locations 8
- *How To Locate a Site* 8
  - Old Landmarks 8
  - Hoot Owl Trees 8
  - Odd Looking Stones 10
  - False Leads 11
  - Universal Signs 11
- *Beware of Armed Sentinels and Booby Traps* 12
- *Maybe More Than Just One Treasure At A Site* 13
- *Letter From a Treasure Hunter* 15

Chapter Three
The Kansas Treasure Site – Found Too Late 17
- *But Source of Much Valuable Information* 17
- *The Man Who Threatened To Shoot My Grandfather* 17
- *A Sentinel Had Been Guarding The Treasure* 18
- *My Search For The Treasure* 18
- *Diamond-Shaped Stones* 18
- *Forked Trees* 19
- *Signs May Point In The Opposite Direction* 19
- *Patterns* 19
- *No two Sites Alike* 20
- *We Find The Treasure Location* 20
- *Was There More Than Just One Treasure Buried Here* 21

About the Author, Dr. Roy William Roush, Ph.D.

Foreword

I have been an active and nationally known treasure hunter for the last 40 years or more, and have written for most of the treasure hunting magazines. Also, I have searched for many kinds of lost and hidden treasures around the United States, Europe, and Mexico, including diving for Spanish treasure off the coasts of California, Florida and Vera Cruz, Mexico.

But the most intriguing and also the one with great possible rewards are the many lost treasures of the mysterious and secret order of the Knights of the Golden Circle in the United States. The Knights were devout southern sympathizers and were very active as a group during and after the Civil War. They were also strongly suspected of being involved in the conspiracy to assassinate President Lincoln.

Because they were not satisfied with how the war ended and deeply resenting the new laws imposed upon them, they decided to go underground and formed a very large secret society with plans to restart the war at a later date. But, they needed financing, so they secretly buried millions of dollars worth of treasure around the country in order to do that when the time came.

Their membership was in the hundreds of thousands and included many people of importance and influence. However, as active and as large as they were, somehow there is no mention of them in our history books today. Consequently, very few people have ever heard of them.

This book is intended to give the reader a better insight into their activities and how to find their treasures. It is my third book on this secretive group--about who they were and why--their secretive and clandestine conspiracy to restart the Civil War--and the vast amount of treasure they accumulated and buried around many parts of our country so they could carry out their plans.

But since they never got around to restarting the Civil War, a lot of their treasures were never recovered and are still there today, making their treasure perhaps the greatest in America (some have estimated the value in the billions of dollars.) Some treasure hunters are now searching throughout the country looking for it, and sometimes finding some of it. I know of at least three of their treasures that have been found, and rumors of several more being found.

My first book about them was The Mysterious and Secret Order of the Knights of the Golden Circle (ISBN: 0-9723072-6-5). It gave some history and background of this group from their beginnings long before the Civil War, during the war and afterwards, plus some information that I had regarding some of their treasure signs and locations.

My second book was How to Find the Treasures of the Knights of the Golden Circle (ISBN: 0-9723072-7-3). It included all of the articles and valuable propitiatory information regarding them and their treasures that originally had been published by Larry Williams for 17 years in the prestigious "Treasure Hunter Confidential Newsletters," plus a couple of chapters that I added from my own information. (Also, I had been co-editor of that newsletter for a number of years before it ceased publication in 2003.)

Those two books are now on my website: knightsofthegoldencircle.net

This book, Knights of the Golden Circle Treasure Signs is mostly a result of some new information and knowledge that I recently acquired when I returned to an old farm in Kansas that my family had once owned to look for a KGC treasure that had been buried there.

Chapter One

WHO WERE THE KNIGHTS OF THE GOLDEN CIRCLE?

As incredible as it may seem, our history books have given us very little, if any, information about the secret and mysterious order of the Knights of the Golden Circle. It is undoubtedly the greatest untold story in American history today.

But, they did exist and were well known during the 1800's because they were very active and were a source of much concern and a threat to our government. Therefore, they received much publicity, mostly criticism, in the newspapers, magazines and periodicals back then. I have copies of some of these stories in my files.

Our government was well aware of their threat and was trying to do something about it, but was having trouble getting any evidence against them because of their extensive secrecy. However, a federal agent by the name of Felix G. Stidger was finally able to infiltrate one of the chapters in Kentucky, became a high-ranking member, and then turned states evidence. As a result, many members of this chapter were arrested and one of the main leaders, Harrison H. Dodd was hanged for treason and conspiracy.

MANY THOUSANDS WERE MEMBERS

Their membership consisted of many thousands of diehard, southern, Confederate rebels and sympathizers of the Confederacy during the Civil War period. Then afterwards, they didn't want to accept what they thought were harsh terms of the surrender. They were still bitter over the slavery issue and of being defeated. The war had been brutal and feelings had run high. They did not want be remain part of the American Union. Instead, they intended to break away and create their own independent country, "The Confederate States of America," and even to also annex part of Mexico.

A lot of important people and community leaders were in this group-- many with much influence. Some of the finest and craftiest brains in the South helped organize and direct their activities. After the war ended, they secretly went underground with a strongly determined and clandestine, even bizarre, plan to eventually restart the war at a later time.

We might think of them as extremist and subversive, but they considered themselves as patriots to an old cause and the way things had been before.

So, maybe that's why we don't want to acknowledge them in our history books today. It just doesn't sound like the American way—it's politically incorrect and seems contrary to what we think of ourselves. But, we all have heard the term "The South shall rise again." Well, they were very serious about it back then.

However, by the time World War One ended in 1918, most of their old members had died out and nobody was interested in fighting another war. Politics were different by then. The South had economically recovered and their cause was being forgotten. Thus began the disintegration of the organization. However, their treasures still remained buried around the country.

PLANS TO RESTART THE CIVIL WAR

Before the Civil War was over, when they realized they were going to lose, is when they secretly decided to start another war...They weren't through yet.

They knew that it would take a lot of money and equipment to finance another war. In fact, they felt that one reason they lost the war was mainly because they ran out of money, and they didn't intend for that to happen again.

HIDING OF TREASURES

So they began to amass a large amount of money and valuables. This was in the nature of gold and silver coins, gold and silver bars, gold nuggets and dust, precious stones and jewelry, but also arms and ammunition which they collected in various ways, including donations, armed robberies and stealing (especially of Northern holdings), skimming of funds, etc.

Many believe that they began with what was left of the Confederate Treasury at the end of the Civil War. Treasure hunters have been looking for years for the missing wagonloads of gold that belonged to the Confederates as it was being moved southward, but was never found.

This was the beginning of their huge treasure trove which they hid in mines and tunnels throughout the country, then covered the entrance. In

other places, holes or huge tunnels were dug, items buried, then cleverly concealed. That happen mostly in the southern part of the United States, especially in the Southeast, but also around gold mining districts in California, Colorado, Arizona, Georgia, and also North Carolina (that prior to California was the largest gold mining district in the United States.) Gold was discovered there in 1799.

DID THE KGC FIND OLD SPANISH TREASURE

Another interesting theory as to where a great amount of their treasure came from is that the KGC were one of the first to look for the old Spanish mines and treasures that had been hidden around the United States, and were also clever enough to find some of them. It is known that the Spanish buried a huge amount of gold that they had mined, then left many treasure signs around so that they could come back for it later, but circumstances intervened and in many cases, they never came back for them.

That could be one explanation as to why so few of the old Spanish treasures have been found by treasure hunters today, even though there are still lots of old Spanish treasure signs and markings around the country.

JESSE AND FRANK JAMES

Another interesting matter concerns the famous outlaws, Jesse James and his brother Frank. It is almost certain that the famed bank and train robbers were members of the KGC, and also donated much of their ill-gotten loot to them. It is known that they were die-hard Confederates and hated the Union, and mostly robbed banks and railroads associated with the North. It has also been said that he and his brother were never big spenders and were not known to live lavishly, even though they got away with hundreds of thousands of dollars. Yet little, if any, of it was ever found or accounted for. If so, that could explain what happened to the money.

But was Jesse James really killed by Bob Ford? There seems to be a lot of doubt about it now among historians and writers today (including myself) mainly due to a number of inconsistencies regarding the story of the shooting...I have always thought the story sounded suspicious.

There are also some questions that have come up regarding the body supposedly buried in the grave of Jesse James. Many now believe that it was the result of a clever scheme in which Bob Ford killed another member of

the gang instead, by the name of Charlie Bigalow, so that Jesse could live on under an assumed name.

It would not have been very difficult to fool the public then because nobody around the area, except his wife, his brother, and a few members of the gang, really knew what Jesse looked like. Therefore, they could have passed off most any similar looking body as that of Jesse James. In fact, the corner had to send for Jesse's mother to come and identify the body, which of course, she was smart enough to say that it was indeed her son.

Some think that he then became a major member of the KGC, using an assumed name.

My first book, The Secret and Mysterious Order of the Knights of the Golden Circle, further explains most of the preceding information with more details

Chapter Two

KGC Treasure Signs and Symbols

Though I have not yet recovered any of their treasures, I have succeeded in discovering two of their sites where I recognized and correctly followed their signs and found where their treasure had once been buried. However, in both cases, the treasure was no longer there--but I have made some careful notes and accumulated much information over the last 30 years that I'll share here with you.

THREE OF THEIR TREASURE SITES

New Mexico

The first site that I discovered was in 1973 at Glorieta Pass, New Mexico. It was at an old historical location where a very large and famous Civil War battle had once occurred. It also was the location of an important stagecoach overnight stop. I was accompanied by my friend Del Schrader and one of his friends who had once been a star quarterback for USC.

Del was the old newspaper reporter in Los Angeles who then wrote his famous book Jesse James Was One of His Names which included information about our trip to Glorieta Pass.

Arkansas

A few years later, I was invited by treasure hunter, Bob Brewer, to visit one of his sites in southwestern Arkansas. It was along an ancient but deserted wagon road and one that he had been working on for some years. He showed me many signs—but, of course, was careful not to show me where he thought the treasure was.

Kansas

Then about 10 years ago, while visiting an old farm in eastern Kansas that my father and his parents had once owned for many years back during the 1930's, I discovered, to my surprise some diamond-shaped stones and bent trees. They were definitely KGC treasure signs and obviously had been there for many years--I'm sure, back to when our family had owned the place, but we had never noticed them. However, I was in a hurry and didn't have time to do a search, but I knew that I would return some day to do that (See next Chapter).

On the property was an old wagon road crossing of a major stream where it spread out over a large, flat, bedrock area. The water here was always shallow and never deep, even at flood stage, so it could be crossed at any time of the year. That location had also served as a popular rest area with lots of good water and timber.

At one time, it had been a branch of the old Santa Fe Trail. It was also very scenic and I'm sure that during pioneer days, it was well known.

I had spent many summers there when I was in grade school, and had become very familiar with the area, but little did we realize then what was buried there.

Favored Locations

Since all three of these sites were at, or near, a landmark or important location of some kind, it occurred to me that the KGC normally selected places like these that were well known during the 1800's. This would include unusual natural formations of some kind, old forts, old houses, old cemeteries, or other old pioneer locations--or maybe even in old caves.

They seemed to prefer rural areas, probably so that they could work more-or-less in secret and not be observed; and also so that the site might not be disturbed later, even though I have heard of some of their treasures being hidden inside of a home, like in the basement, cellar or attic. There is also a report of one in a filled-in cellar in Texas.

The KGC also selected locations around gold mining areas, like in California, Colorado, Arizona, New Mexico and also in North Carolina and Georgia.

In these areas, they also could use existing mine tunnels or shafts to bury their treasures in, and due to the large space available, they usually buried guns, cannons, black powder, or other military equipment here. But I wouldn't bother to dig unless there were definitely KGC treasure signs around it.

HOW TO LOCATE A SITE

Old Landmarks

If you decide to go searching for a KGC treasure, it would be a good idea to start near an old landmark or unusual formation of some kind that I have just described that normally would be away from a populated area.

For those who may be researching old maps or records, keep in mind that some names might have changed by now.

Hoot Owl Trees

The first thing that you might notice could be a bent or unusual looking tree, or trees (referred to as "Hoot Owl" trees), especially where there are three or more in a straight line and of equal distance apart. They were mainly put there so the site could be recognized from a distance--if you were the right person, but to be overlooked by others. All of these bent, bowed or deformed trees were made that way when they were quite small when they could easily be worked on or grafted together or replanted.

Then, you need to search the area near the trees for the key signs, markers, or lines-of-sight that could tell you exactly where the treasure is buried. Normally, these will be unusual looking stones, some shaped like arrows or pointers, or diamond-shaped, or maybe holes that have been drilled into rocks or trees—most anything that is not natural.

No two treasure sites are alike or have the same pattern or arrangement of signs, mainly because of differences in the terrain, but also because anyone solving one could then easily find the others.

Generally their layout was something like this: First, they put up something to mark the area that could easily be seen, like bent or deformed trees, then they scattered odd-shaped stones or other objects around the area--some of which should be the key signs, and if figured out correctly, will lead you to the exact spot where to dig. Also, the treasure will normally be located somewhere near the center of all the signs.

But, keep in mind that some of the signs could be missing, or might have been altered by graffiti after all these years. Also, the site might not be in the same condition or arrangement as it originally was due to natural erosion or land developments. Maybe by now, it could be next to someone's backyard.

Also remember that sometimes the treasure is no longer there, but the signs are still there, because if the treasure is gone, why would anybody take the trouble to eliminate the signs around it?

If you find three trees or more in a straight row that are approximately of the same size and of equal distance apart, that should be a KGC sign. And if you happen to notice that one seems to be missing--that could be where the treasure is.

That was the situation at Glorieta Pass in New Mexico. The treasure had been buried where three old trees were in an exact row, but there was a missing space between the second and third tree where another tree should have been too make them all equally spaced--that was the spot. However, the treasure had just recently been washed out by a flash flood, and a person living nearby accidentally found it.

I also discovered a 4-inch diameter hole nearby that was drilled into the side of a huge rock that was pointing exactly in line towards the three large trees. And when I found it, it helped to point out where the treasure had been buried. It also served as a permenant back up in case one or more of the trees were no longer there.

It is of interest to me that I did not notice any diamond-shaped stones at Glorieta Pass, although I had been told to look for anything that was not natural which would be the treasure signs. Even though, I did notice the bent tree, the face carved on the side of a big rock, and the 4-inch-diameter hole drilled into the side of it as a pointer, I'm sure the stones must have been there, but were so subtle that they went unnoticed by me and also the other two people.

The arrangement of those trees and the hole in the rock is described in my recent book, The Mysterious and Secret Order of The Knights of The Golden Circle.

Odd Looking Stones

As I have said, that in addition to the bent or deformed trees, or trees in a straight row, there should be numerous diamond-shaped stones or other man-shaped stones scattered around the area--maybe up to 20 or more, including some shaped like arrow heads, or faces (especially a smiling face), or maybe there are rocks or trees with holes drilled in them, or with other unusual markings... or anything NOT NATURAL that could probably go unnoticed by the casual passerby.

Then somewhere among them, there should be an arrangement, or combination of signs, using the rocks and/or trees, to show you where the treasure is buried. But, of course, recognizing which ones they are and what they mean is the most difficult and essential part.

An individual sign by itself will not tell you where the treasure is. It will only be part of the overall puzzle. This means that anyone (including a KGC member) has to use logic, skill, ingenuity, and judgment, to find where the treasure is buried.

But usually, there are more than just one major sign or key marker to indicate exactly where the treasure is buried. That also acts as insurance because if there was just one key marker and it some how got obliterated, removed, destroyed or changed, then there probably would be no way for sure to find the treasure later on—especially if something were to happen to the Sentinel who was always guarding it. Also, duplication would make it a bit easier to find the treasure when they decided to recover it.

I have no reason to believe that you have to locate all of the signs first, then follow each one (going from one to the next) in a special sequence to lead you to where the treasure is buried.

Rarely, if ever, will there be a marker or an "X" exactly on top of the treasure. In many cases, you need to use the line-of-sight method and measure out distances to find where the treasure is, or sometimes it is where two lines-of-sight cross.

Once, I saw what was obviously a fake gravestone in Arkansas with cryptic writing on it. But please—do not disturb any gravesites. The gravestone only had information on it and was not placed over where the treasure had been buried.

A bent or bowed tree should point in the general direction of where you should go next. But remember that these trees may be old and maybe one or two may not be there anymore.

However, I noticed that at the Arkansas site and also at the Kansas site, there were some bowed trees that were somewhat small and did not seem to be very old. In these cases, I believe the Sentinels had replaced some of the old trees that had fallen with newer ones. Apparently, the Sentinels were not only obligated to guard the treasure, but also to maintain the treasure signs. And, there is reason to believe that the KGC were still active and burying their treasures up to about the end of the century.

False Leads

None of the sites that I have been to were easy to solve. Sometimes, there are false leads to confuse you. Some of the signs, including arrows or pointers, are purposely pointing in the opposite direction intending to lead someone in the wrong direction. It would probably help to put yourself in their place and try to think as they would have at the time. Normally, It will take hours, or even days to figure them out.

Sometimes a fake hole was made, then covered up so as to be noticeable to attract the attention of any treasure hunter looking for the treasure. This would be watched by the Sentinel as he made his rounds, and if there were any sign of digging, he would set up an ambush later to shoot the intruder.

Universal Signs

The Spanish used treasure signs that pretty much meant the same thing in order to lead them back to their treasure sites, but few of the KGC treasure signs were universal, except for the bent, bowed or deformed trees, and the diamond-shaped rocks that could be recognized by fellow KGC members as KGC treasure signs. From there on, it was left to the ability and skill of the person, or persons, who was supposed to recover it to figure out what the various signs meant.

The KGC sometimes followed the same idea used by Pirates in the old days of burying their treasures in a rather large and deep hole that took a number of people to do, and consequently about the same number to recover it, thereby making it difficult and very time consuming for just one person to go back alone and recover the treasure without being discovered by the Sentinel who assigned to guard the area.

I don't believe that there was ever a master listing of all of the sites with information on how to correctly read the signs. But I do believe that each Castle, or regional group, did have some cryptic notations or references as to where the sites were in their area and the approximate value of each. Only in that way could they keep track of the total value of their treasures around the country. This they needed to know so that they would know how soon they could restart the Civil War.

If you are looking in a natural cave for some of their treasure, I would believe that the key sign, or signs, to look for would be holes drilled into the sides. And if any lines-of-sight intersect, that should indicate where the treasure is buried.

Since their signs and treasures might possibly be located almost anywhere, but more likely in areas where there are trees, keep your eyes open wherever you might go, especially if you are treasure hunting.

In fact, just a few weeks ago, I discovered a diamond-shaped stone in a box of relics that I had picked up years ago while treasure hunting somewhere in California (or was it in Nevada…or maybe Arizona?) At the time, I just thought it was a rather unusual looking stone. Now, I am scratching my head trying to figure out where it was that I had found it. So again, like the farm in Kansas, treasure was under my feet and I didn't know it!

BEWARE OF ARMED SENTINELS AND BOOBY TRAPS

Sentinels were armed and dangerous and were assigned to guard each treasure site, under threat of death if they failed. However, after the end of World War One in 1918, some of them began to disappear, although some were still around later on—including one who was still guarding the site on our old farm in Kansas during the early 1930's. He threatened to shoot my grandfather if he tried to change our fence line to where it should have been. (See next chapter.)

I'm sure that there was much consternation going on then among the surviving members and Sentinels as to what to do next, since communications were probably breaking down and membership was declining, making them wonder if the Knights of the Golden Circle were still active, or not? Since Sentinels were under the threat of death if they removed the treasure themselves, or revealed its location, other than to assigned the duties to a another Sentinel (usually a family member), should they take a chance on recovering the treasure themselves, or were there still plans to start another Civil War, or not?

It must have been a big temptation for them to get rich quick - but what if they got caught? They realized that possibly they were still being secretly watched by other members, or by the Ku Klux Klan, which was the militant arm of the Knights of the Golden Circle. I believe that eventually some Sentinels decided to take a chance to recover the treasure, while others died and took the secret with them to the grave. So, there are still many KGC treasures out there to be found.

But, don't forget that it is possible that some are still being guarded by a die-hard, third or fourth generation Sentinel who still believes the treasure should be guarded; or maybe someone else who is armed and dangerous, such as a relative of a Sentinel who wants to guard the treasure for himself. Or maybe it could be someone still looking for it who wants to keep everybody else away from the site. I have heard of some really amazing stories about shootings and gunplay over situations involving buried treasure—even among friends.

Another word of caution! Keep in mind that there have been reports of some treasure sites that have been booby-trapped in the nature of explosions, pitfalls, water traps, landslides, and cave-in's that have been fatal to some treasure hunters.

MAYBE MORE THAN JUST ONE TREASURE AT A SITE

Another important point to keep in mind is that it is believed there were usually more than just one treasure buried at a site - maybe up to three or four, or more. This is where the KGC Map Circle Overlay might be used, like the one on the cover of my previous book How To Find The Treasures of The Knights of The Golden Circle.

I realize that some people may be skeptical about the KGC and their treasures, or maybe think that it was all the work of just a few people, or a very small group…Well, absolutely not! Just considering the three sites that I have been to, and the great number of man-shaped stones that I have seen and photographed, it would have been too much for a small group to do. And don't forget that these three sites were in three different states hundreds of miles apart. Additionally, times were hard back then, and people didn't have much time to waste on insignificant things. The signs speak for themselves that they were something of importance, involving much time and hard work from a lot of people around the country.

None of their treasure will ever be easy to find. They were meant to be that way. It will take concentration, effort, imagination, luck and some time to be successful. Also, you will need good medal detecting equipment, the experience and the skill to use them properly. Although some of the treasures are gone by now, there are still many out there to be found by those with the right knowledge and equipment.

LETTER FROM A TREASURE HUNTER

The following is a letter I recently received from a KGC Treasure Hunter that might be helpful that I have permission to include, but his name is being withheld by request:

Dear Roy

Enclosed please find my check for $24.95 as payment for your book "How to Find the Treasures of the KGC".

One thought on your family farm. Next time you're there, back check the line that took you to the hole. There may be more caches along that line, just like the KGC compasses show. Go all the way back to the first sign, and further until you don't see a sign. Measure the distance, and then follow the line past the hole that distance. You might find more clues along the way leading you to another cache. They were laid out on equal distances. Metal detect maybe 3 feet each side of the line to check for buried clues. Its strange there would only be one cache there, if it had a sentinel on it. There should be more.

Another thing I discovered is to dig at the base below marked trees, maybe 4-8 inches deep. There are sometimes rock clues left there, pointers showing you a new line or trail marker. I once found three flat stones, set up as "faux" gravestones. Beneath each was a carved rock clue. Two of them gave me small carved hearts. The third, a pointer rock. The G-stones were in a triangle, and there should have been a cache in the middle. We used one of Fitz's machines, and the signal kept fading away. I figured I had hit a residual. Then found out later some other folks were "testing" their machine in the same area. But they didn't find anything. Right.

I finished your first book today. Some good info in there. Maybe some time you could point me to that NM Master Compass treasure guide rock.

Good luck and Good hunting.

Chapter Three

THE KANSAS TREASURE SITE – FOUND TOO LATE

BUT SOURCE OF MUCH VALUABLE INFORMATION

As I mentioned in the last chapter that about 10 years ago, I accidentally discovered some KGC treasure signs while visiting an old farm in eastern Kansas that my father and his parents had once owned during the 1930's. What I saw was a bent tree and some diamond-shaped stones. But I was in a hurry and didn't have time to do a search then…However, I knew that someday I would return to do that.

Well, recently, I got that opportunity when my brother and I returned with metal detectors to search for the treasure. But we had to get permission first since the land is now under new ownership.

We found many KGC signs, followed them, and thought we were going to find a big treasure. And we would have, except that at the end ,all we found a very large and empty hole—some one had already dug it up years ago.

Even though we were very disappointed at not finding the treasure, the site was still extremely valuable, because there was a bonanza of information that I learned from it. It was a great education on how the KGC laid out this treasure site, the various treasure signs they left around it, and what the signs meant. This was because having found where the treasure had once been buried, most of the signs leading to it were still there--which now I understand. This indeed was a very rare and unique opportunity.

That was the second time I had seen, recognized their signs, and followed them to where their treasure had once been buried. This has helped me a great deal to understand their thinking and how they set up their treasure sites.

THE MAN WHO THREATENED TO SHOOT MY GRANDFATHER

Those of you who have read my recent book The Mysterious and Secret Order of The Knights of the Golden Circle will probably remember in the last chapter where I wrote about the man who had threatened to shoot my grandfather back in the 1930's if he tried to change our fence line to enclose a small corner of a wooded area on this farm. Up till then, a small corner of my father's property was not inside his fence line—and that's where the treasure had been buried.

But at the time, there seemed to be absolutely no explanation as to why he would be so threatening since he lived across the road from it and his property did not adjoin ours. Although it's possible that it might have been in the past before a new road was put through the area in about 1915 which could have separated the properties.

The situation was resolved a few months later when my father, who had been a cowboy in his early years at Dodge City, arrived in the area from Oklahoma City where we lived--announced that he was going to change the fence to where it should be and anybody showing up with a gun, would be shot.

I still vividly remember the day. My father carried his trusty old

30-30 semi-automatic rifle and his old six-shooter, while my grandfather carried his old 12-guage, double-barreled shotgun, and I went along with my BB gun. The man never showed himself, maybe thinking that he was out-gunned.

A SENTINEL HAD BEEN GUARDING THE TREASURE

Little did we ever realize then that the man was undoubtedly the Sentinel who had been assigned to guard a KGC treasure that was on that little piece of land. At that time, nobody had ever heard of the KGC, let alone, that they had buried treasures around the country.

MY SEARCH FOR THE TREASURE

After going to the Annual Texas Treasure Hunter's Show in March 2007 that I usually attend each year and give a presentation on treasure hunting, I had the opportunity to go back there with my brother who lives in Dallas, and who is also involved in treasure hunting. That experience greatly expanded my knowledge of the KGC treasures and understanding of their signs.

DIAMOND-SHAPED STONES

When we arrived, we parked the car along the road, then we headed towards the corner of the land that had originally been fenced off, since logic told me it had to be where the treasure was. But along the way, we began to see many diamond-shaped stones scattered about. They ranged from large ones about 2 feet long to smaller ones about 7 inches long. (See the photographs at the end of this chapter.)

The first one we noticed was a rather large one right under the fence at the roadside. However, as I have already mentioned, the road was put in some years after the treasure had been buried. The stone was about 200 yards from where the treasure had been buried. But it may not have been the farthest out. I suspect that there were more farther away. Normally, their treasure should be buried approximately in the middle of all of the signs.

Next, I noticed a very thick stone about 14 inches long and about 10 inches thick and of an irregular shape, except that the top was very flat and even. It looked like it had been polished smooth (see photo). It somewhat resembled an arrowhead and it did point towards the corner of the land that had originally been fenced off.

FORKED TREES

After that, I noticed two forked trees arranged so that if they were used like a gun sight, they would also point in the direction of the corner. These trees, like others in the area, appeared to have been grafted together when they were quite small many years ago. Forked trees are not very common in the area, especially if the fork is at the bottom as if they were twin trees.

Then I noticed six more trees, all of equal distance apart. They apparently had been planted there in a straight line. The first and third trees also were forked, and when I stood at the first tree and looked down the line, they pointed in the direction of where the treasure had been buried.

SIGNS MAY POINT IN THE OPPOSITE DIRECTION

However, if I stood at the other end and looked, they pointed away from the treasure. The same was true with most of the diamond-shaped stones. The alignment of their pointed ends either pointed towards the treasure, or in the opposite direction. But, not always. I noticed that some of the stones were not aligned and were pointing off to other directions. Perhaps they were positioned that way so that it would not be too noticeable, rather than if they all pointed the same way.

Also, I'd like to point out that some of their other signs, such as arrows, arrowhead's or pointers, were purposely pointing in the opposite direction of where the treasure was to throw off and confuse someone hunting for the treasure.

Another forked tree nearby had a strange looking, hollowed-out stump next to it. I was not quite sure as to the meaning of it, except to realize that it was made by the KGC to draw attention to the area.

I also noticed that the diamond-shaped rocks were usually placed out by themselves and not in amongst other rocks--which meant of course, they had not broken off of an adjoining rock, but had carefully been placed there to be noticed. And usually the sharp ends were aligned in the direction of the treasure, or away from it, so you have to work on it to find which direction you are supposed to follow.

PATTERNS

Their patterns seem to be that large signs, like bent or bowed trees, or large faces carved on the side of a big rock, or cliff sides that are visible from a distance, were used to help zero in on the location. Then, the smaller shaped rocks were used to get the finder closer to the location. And finally, various subtle items, such as markings, drilled holes, or something missing that should be there, were left as clues to be solved.

NO TWO SITES ALIKE

However, the method used to solve one treasure site would probably not work at another site. Each location was unique and one has to use logic, ingenuity, imagination, skill and lots of luck to find the buried treasure. There was never an "X" marking the spot over a treasure, nor probably anything else directly over it.

Now I must emphasize that "yes," sometimes you can find or notice a bent tree or two here and there, and also some peculiar shaped stones or other signs that could be a coincidence of nature and not shaped by humans. And that is exactly what the clever KGC intended--to hide things in plain sight so as not to be noticed unless you were part of their group...a very, very, clever and workable plan indeed. But, when you find the signs repeatedly in one area, that is no coincidence.

It's interesting that their method could work without any detailed maps ever being made of it, such as here and at the Glorieta Pass treasure

site. I doubt if there ever was a detailed map of any of the treasure sites, because a map could easily be stolen one way or another over the many years that these treasures were buried (which was approximately from the end of the Civil War in 1885, to around the end of the century, or a little more.)

However, I'm sure there were secret references or listing of the landmarks at each Castle (headquarters) for that area, since the treasure was also probably collected and buried by the members of that group. I believe that most treasures originated within each group's territory and not hauled for some distance to be buried at another spot. And I would imagine that there was competition between the groups to see who could come up with the biggest treasures.

As we got closer to where the treasure had been buried, I began to see some rectangular, almost square-shaped, stones. Later, I realized that they were telling me that I should look for a rectangular shaped formation nearby. We were getting close, and proceeded on.

WE FIND THE TREASURE LOCATION

Next, I saw three signs close together, as shown in one of the photographs. One was a rectangular-shaped stone very close to the base of a twin tree that was joined at the base to form a "V" (another gun site). There was also a very strange looking stone nearby that was shaped like a harpoon and pointing towards the stone and the tree. The three items were aligned, also as shown in one of the photographs. The shape and positioning of these rocks I considered positively not something of a natural occurrence, but of human origin. It was the main key to finding the treasure, and when I stood in line with the rocks and the tree and looked through the fork in the tree, like a gun site, I could see a very large hole about 20 feet beyond where the treasure had been dug up many years before. Only a few of the rocks that had been part of the old rectangular foundation were left

The hole was approximately 8-by-10 feet in size and about 3 feet deep. The hole had been somewhat deeper at one time, but it had been dug up at least 20 or 30 years ago, possibly using a backhoe, and it had partly been filled back in. I'm almost positive that the one who recovered it was the Sentinel who had lived across the road and the one who had threatened to shoot my grandfather. Or else maybe it was his son, or some one related to him.

I quickly recognized the location. It was where a very small cabin or shack had once stood over a foundation made of loose stones. I had played around it many times when I was a child. It was in a rather remote and hidden location here in the timber, and I had always wondered why it was there. Nothing was left then in the early 1930's except some stones of the foundation and a couple of old boards. It seemed to be out of place there in the timber all by itself with no sign of anything else around it. I often wondered who might have lived there or what it was used for. Now, I know!

The treasure had been under the floor and maybe it was where the first Sentinel had once lived for a while. Then the treasure was left there long after the shack fell apart feet!

Oh, if only I had known then that treasure was actually under my

WAS THERE MORE THAN JUST ONE TREASURE BURIED HERE

I have heard that usually there are more than just one treasure buried at a site, but we were getting short on time, and besides, it was beginning to rain, and since we needed to get back to Dallas that night, we headed for home.

However, I'm keeping the place in mind and plan to go back to check it out more thoroughly…and maybe even around the old ruins of the Sentinel's house across the road, in case he buried some of it there after he recovered the treasure.

Even though I didn't find this treasure, I still consider the experience valuable, due to all the treasure signs I saw, and since I positively found where the treasure had been, I am now able to recognize and understand what the signs meant. It was a great education.

More information on the treasure signs and symbols of the KGC can be found in my first two books: The Mysterious and Secret Order of the Knights of the Golden Circle, and How to Find the Treasures of the Knights of the Golden Circle. See the web site: knightsofthegoldencircle.net

Good Luck--and I hope that this information will make it possible for some of you to find your fortune...And remember, always keep your eyes open for their signs wherever you might go!

The author is shown here at his table during a recent Treasure Hunters Show in Texas. The show is sponsored annually by the Texas Council of Treasure Clubs. The author is shown here at his table during a recent Treasure Hunters Show in Texas. The show is sponsored annually by the Texas Council of Treasure Clubs.

This is on an old farm in Kansas that my Dad once owned in the 1930's where I discovered KGC treasure signs a few years ago. It once had been a branch of the old Santa Fe Trail where the river flows over a large, flat bedrock area. Wagons could cross the river here at any time since the water was never deep, and it was an excellent place to stop and rest and to water the horses and cattle.

This is a first KGC treasure sign that we noticed at the old Kansas farm-a very large, man-shaped rock about 18 in. long and right at the fence line along the road. It was probably placed here before the road was made, then the fence was installed over it. It was about 150 yd. from the treasure and has been a.re undisturbed for maybe 100 years or more.

Side view of the first stone that we found. Notice how straight, smooth and even the left side is. They could have made all four sides more perfectly, but that would be too obvious.

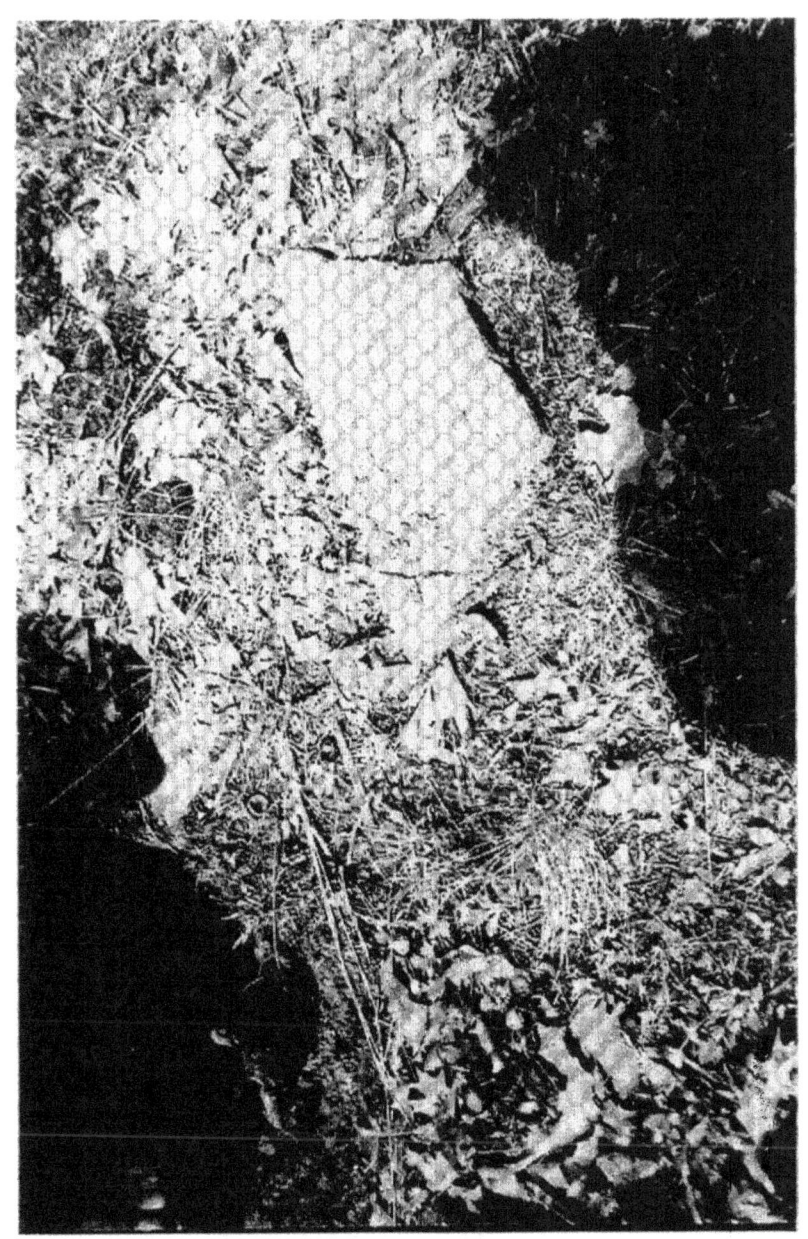

View of the underside of the stone to see if there were any inscriptions. In this case, there wasn't any.

As we progressed further towards where the treasure had been, we found this stone which was quite noticeably very smooth and flat on top. It also appeared to be in the shape of an arrowhead and was pointing in the right direction. It was different from any I had ever seen before, and I'm not sure what it meant, except maybe to look for a flat area that had been cleared off; and if so, then it would have been the flat and smooth area where the old shack had been.

About 50 feet from the fence line, were these two trees that had been grafted together when they were quite small. I realized later that if one stood where the diamond shaped rock was at the fence line and sighted through the fork of the tree, that was the direction where the treasure had been buried.

Another diamond shaped stone, but larger than most of the rest. It obviously had been here many years before we pulled it loose to take this picture.

This stone closely resembles the shape of the Masonic Emblem. A lot of the KGC members were also members of the Masonic Lodge. It is rather typical in size, shape and proportion to most of their rocks. It is an obvious sign to an experienced KCG treasure hunter, but not to anyone else, and that is exactly what they intended.

This rock, found at the Arkansas site in 1997, is almost the exact shape of the Masonic Emblem. Compare it to the photo on the previous page of a rock found at the Kansas site.

Then we came to this unusual twin tree (two trees sharing a single base.) They were probably grafted together when they were much smaller. Also of interest is the hollowed-out stump next to it which could indicate that something was buried nearby in a hole.

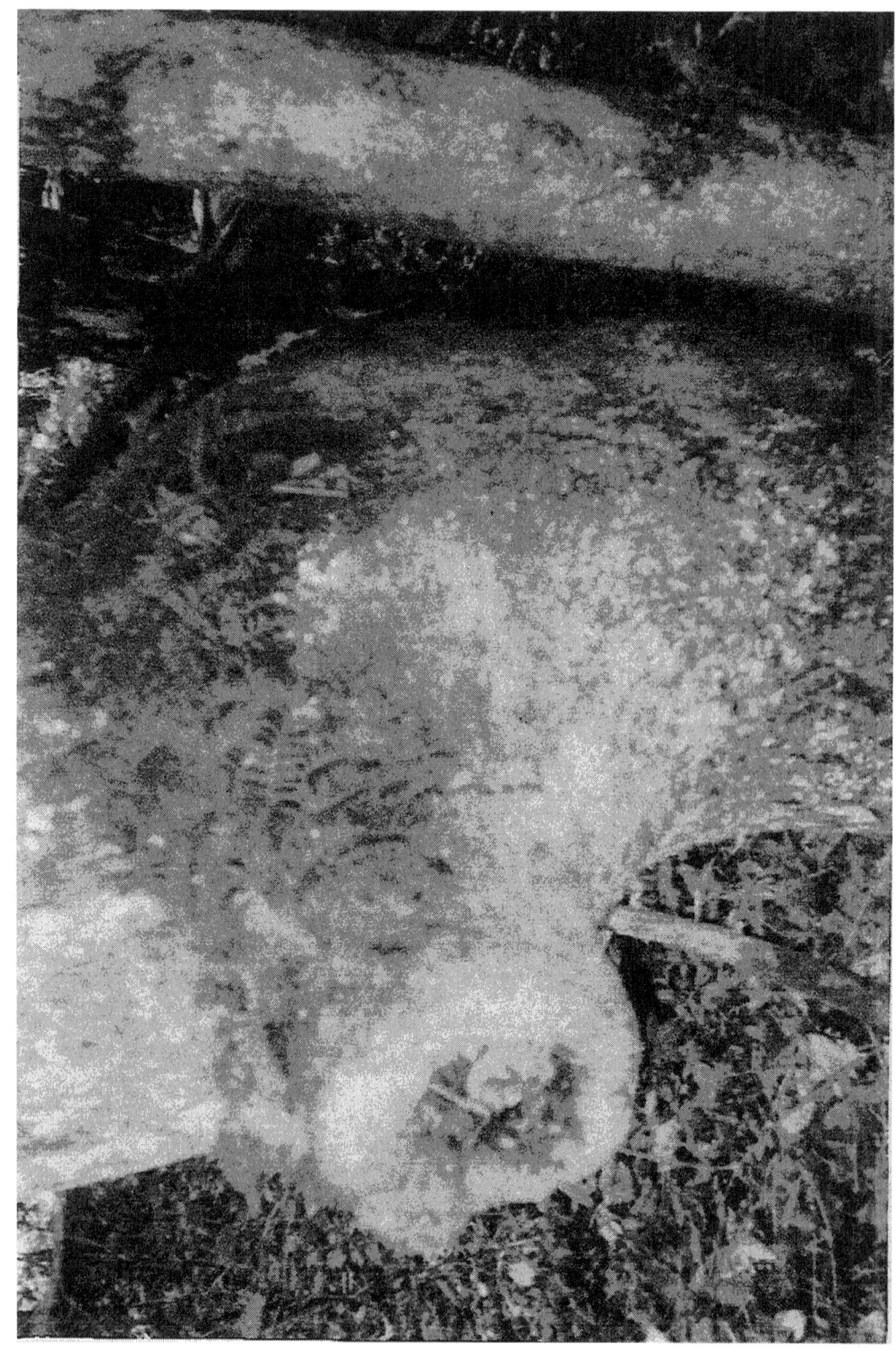

This tree at the Arkansas site also shows a hollowed out stump, indicating that treasure is buried in a hole nearby and probably in the direction it is pointing.

Two more diamond shaped rocks close to each other. They put numerous signs around their sites so that years later, it would not be too difficult for the KGC to find them. I'm sure there were quite a few more treasure signs around that we didn't see because we walked in pretty much of a straight line to where the treasure had been and didn't bother to follow a trail of signs.

Another forked tree (two trees that had been grafted together when they were small) that I realized had been made by the KGC. I'm sure that there were more of these around that we didn't pass by.

As we progressed, we saw these six trees all in a straight line and of equal distance apart, in line with the treasure site. And two of them have forks. They are obviously a KGC treasure sign and about 300 feet from the treasure site. Again, it is an example of how they hid their signs in plain sight.

This stone is almost too obvious. However, it still went unnoticed by myself and the rest of my family, although we must have stepped over it many times. But even if we had noticed it, we could have never guessed what it meant. The KGC members were diabolical clever and hid their signs In plain sight, yet they went unnoticed.

This is by far the largest of the shaped stones that we saw. It was about four or five feet long and does not fit in with the rocks around it. Again, noticed how straight and smooth one side of it is. I'm sure that it must have taken many hours to make it like this. It is difficult to imagine how many people must have been involved in this project alone, plus the many other treasure sites they had around the country.

Another example of a KGC treasure sign rock. Notice that at least one side, and often two (such as seen here and in other photos) are almost perfectly straight and smooth. That is a giveaway to it being a KGC treasure sign rock. Also notice that they have one end that is sharp and pointed.

This rather large rock is obviously a pointer, and in fact, was pointing in the direction of the treasure site. It was different and I don't recall seeing one like this anywhere else before.

Another stone that is very typical in shape and proportion to most of their other stones. From the number of stones we saw here (and there had to be many more that we didn't see), it must have taken many men many days to make all these rocks and treasure signs, which indicates this treasure must have been very big and important.

Here is another grafted tree. It's true that sometimes this does occur in nature, but it is rather rare. At this site, there were more than a normal amount of these, and in most cases, they could be used like a gun sight to either point you towards the treasure site, or away from it. So, you had to figure out which direction to go.

Still another typical example of one of their man-shaped stones, setting out by itself and away from any other rocks--yet we had never noticed it before either. Judging from the number of the stones that we saw, I would estimate that there were at least 30 or more of the shaped stones and a dozen or more of their trees around the area that we didn't see.

Another KGC treasure rock. Notice the tip of my rubber boot in the lower right hand corner for a comparison of size. There were quite a few more shaped rocks that we saw and photographed, but didn't include In this book since they were typical of the ones already shown in the these photographs.

There are three KGC treasure rocks plainly visible in this photo, and maybe one more at the bottom. One thing to remember is that they don't always point towards the treasure. I think their purpose was mainly as markers around a treasure site so that it would be easier to locate in the future. Remember, back then, most of these locations were very remote.

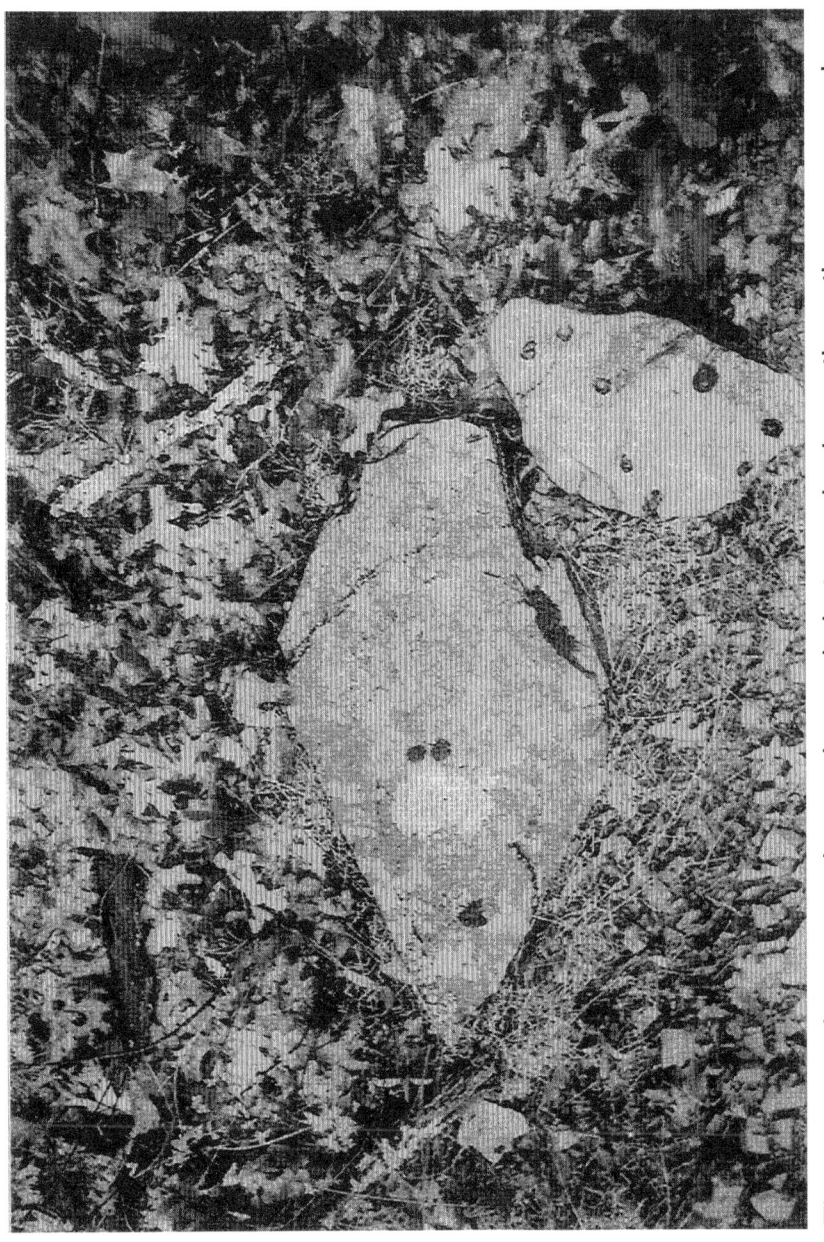

These two rocks are very interesting and photographed exactly as they were one has three holes drilled in it and is in the shape of a smiling fish. The other has seven holes in it which could mean that seven treasures were buried in the area. I have often heard that usually more than just one treasure is buried at a site, which makes a lot of sense. A smiling rock is a good sign and I encountered two of them before in 1973 at one of their sites at Glorieta Pass in New Mexico.

As we got pretty close to the site, we saw these two rocks placed on top of a huge rock, which coincidentally, also points in the right direction. I'm sure that the rectangular one means to look for something rectangular to find the treasure (which had been buried inside the rectangular pattern of the stone foundation of the old shack.) This is a typical example of how they used signs that had a meaning for you to figure out.

Here are three KGC treasure signs very close to the treasure site. The one that is very noticeable on top of the big rock is pointing towards the treasure, but the other two or more rectangular, which I later realize meant to look for a rectangular pattern ahead, and indeed that is where the treasure had been. It is interesting to note that they had redundant signs around.

This is a close-up of a very definitely, man-shaped rectangular rock that was shown in the previous photo. Noticed how almost perfectly it has been shaped. I never cease to be amazed at how meticulous these men were.

This is the underside of the rectangular rock shown in the last photograph. Sometimes they left markings or additional information on the bottom side of their rocks, but not in this case. Again, notice how carefully the rock has been shaped.

Then, as we got within about 40 feet from where the treasure had been, we saw these three treasure signs. On the right is obviously a man-shaped stone like a pointer, but in this case is pointing in the opposite direction--as sometimes they did. Then, there was a rectangular stone placed near the trunk of a twin tree.

Here is the main and final key to the treasure. You need to look through the fork of the tree from this position for something close by that is rectangular. In this case, it was the rectangular stone foundation where the old cabin had been that I first saw in about 1930, and had played around it when I was in grade school. You can actually see the empty hole in the background.

A huge, shallow hole now marks the place were the treasure had been dug up many years ago, after we had sold the land in about 1943. Apparently, someone had used a backhoe to recover the treasure. Judging from the size of the hole, the treasure must have been huge. It is my opinion that it was recovered by the Sentinel who had lived across the road nearby, or perhaps someone else In his family.

Here is a close-up of the pointer rock. Again, notice how smooth and straight the sides are and also the very sharp corners. There is no way that nature could have shaped the stone this way. It would be very noticeable for a KGC member to recognize it later as a treasure sign.

Many years too late... This is the author searching around the hole with a metal detector to see if anything was left, but there wasn't. However, one of the stones of the old foundation is shown here.

This unusual looking tree was just to the right of the empty hole (part of which can be seen at the bottom of the picture.) The left branch stuck out over where the treasure had been buried. It was another redundant sign to indicate where the treasure was, like a waving arm. And notice the sharp bend in the right branch. It did not grow naturally this way.

This is my brother, Donald, who is also searching, but had no luck ether. If only I had known in the 1930s what I know now, we could have been fabulously rich.... but then again, it could have ended in a violent gun battle with the Sentinel across the road who had been closely guarding it and had once threatened to shoot my grandfather if he changed the fence line to include that piece of land.

This is the bent tree that I first discovered while visiting the Kansas site in 1997. It and some diamond-shaped stones nearby, indicated to me that a KGC treasure was buried nearby. But I didn't have time then to search for it, however I knew that I would someday, and in March of 2007 I did, but only found a big empty hole.

These are some on the KGC treasure stones that we picked up as souvenirs and brought back to Dallas. They now unadorned my brothers front yard.

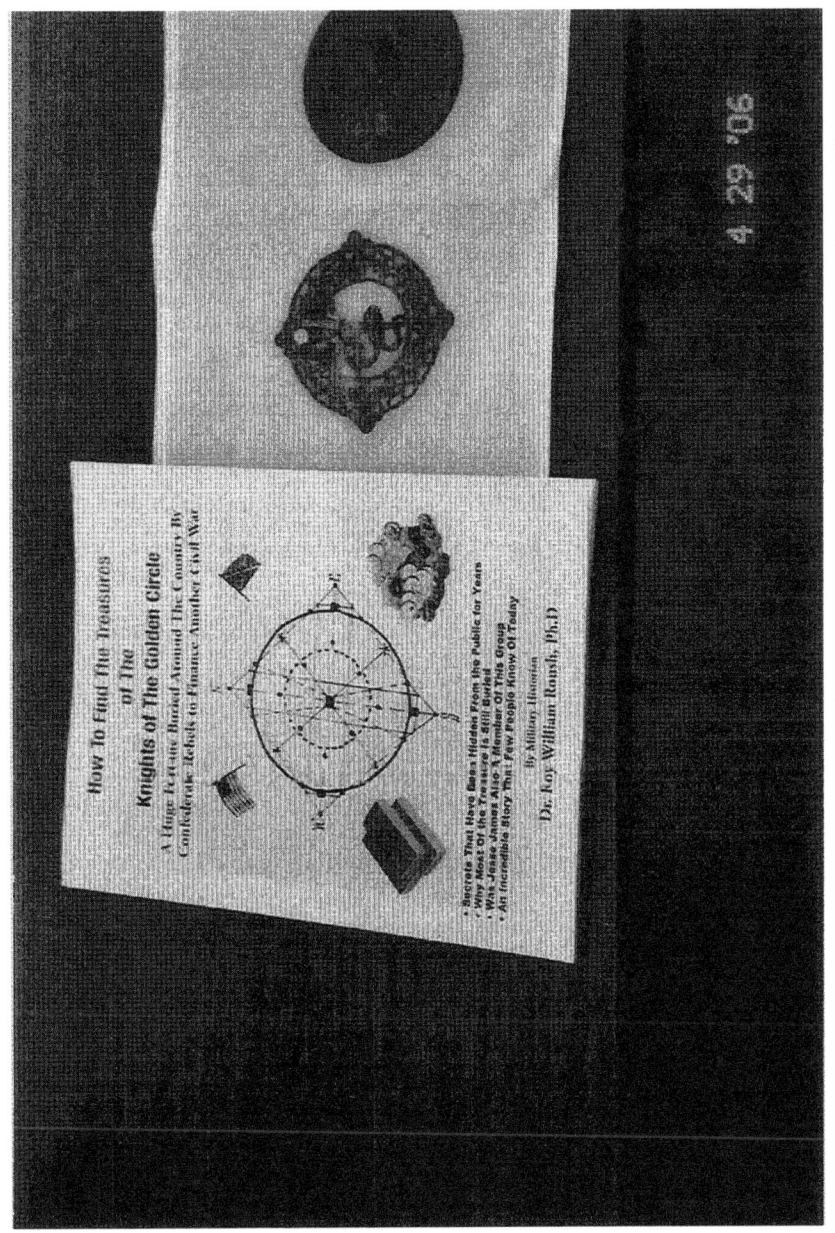

This interesting photo was taken in 2006 at the Fort Worth Treasure Show. Someone came to my table with the item shown in the middle that he had found with a metal detector. It was about 2 inches across, and we concluded that it was a KGC Pocket Piece. Notice how closely it resembles the KGC Treasure Map Overlay shown on the front cover of my last book. The photo of it and the large penny next to it is an enlargement.

The author is shown here at the Glorieta Pass, New Mexico site in 1973 examining a 'Smiling Rock' (a KGC treasure sign) that is pointing to where the treasure had once been buried. When the KGC used a face as one of their signs, it usually wore a smile and also was looking in the direction where the treasure was.

This unusual looking tree in the sign of a cross, along with two bent trees, were seen at the Arkansas site along the old abandoned wagon road. They were intended to attract attention and seem to indicate that the treasure is buried in the direction they are pointing.

Another deformed tree, photographed at the Arkansas site in 1997, is one of the most unusual I have ever seen. Trees never grow naturally this way and it was a sure sign that KGC treasure was buried nearby.

This stone, also photographed at the Arkansas site, is the largest diamond-shaped stone I have ever seen. It was about 3 ft. long and perfectly proportioned. Notice how almost perfectly smooth and straight the top and sides are. It took a lot of work to make it this way.

The author is shown here on the left holding his highly sensitive and deep seeking VP-200 metal detector at Glorieta Pass, New Mexico in 1973. When only told to look for anything "not natural" to locate the site, this deformed 'Hoot Owl' tree was the first thing noticed. The tree had obviously been deformed by the KGC when it was quite small. It leaned towards where the treasure had been.

Here are some more KGC treasure stones that my brother picked up when he went back to the Kansas farm site again to see if maybe there was another treasure buried there – In case we missed it the first time, but no luck. There are still more of these stones scattered around the area. Notice the one in the lower right corner…. How much more obvious could it be that it was put there as a pointer rock? sometimes, it's not too difficult to figure out where their treasure is buried once you find a site.

About the Author, Dr. Roy William Roush, Ph.D.

The author is one of. the most recognized names in the world as an authority on the subject of Treasure Hunting and Gold Prospecting for over 40 years. He has also been very active in those fields and has served as a researcher and consultant for a number of organizations and individuals, plus organizing and participating in treasure expeditions and underwater salvage projects in the Florida Keys, the Bahamas, Turks and Caicos Islands, Mexico, Puerto Rico, and Europe, as well as throughout the United States.

Obtaining a B.A. Degree in Journalism in 1950, he used his journalism expertise to write for many of the Treasure Hunting Publications including: "Treasure," "Treasure Hunter," "Treasure Search," "Treasure Found," and "Treasure News." Later, he earned a Ph.D. in Archaeology.

He also fought with the US Marines in World War II during the battles of Guadalcanal, Tarawa, Saipan, and Tinian in the South Pacific as a front-line combat rifleman. Then, during the Korean War, he flew Jet Fighters and F-51 Mustang's as an officer with the U.S. Air Force. Recently, he authored a major book about his experiences in combat and as an Air Force fighter pilot, entitled "OPEN FIRE." (Website OPEN-FIRE.US)

Being one of the first to use a metal detector in the early 1960's (building his first one in 1962), he has searched for many of the well-know lost treasures, including: the Lost Dutchman; the 17 Tons of Mexican Gold in New Mexico; Peg Leg's Black Gold Nuggets; Iron Door Mine; Knights of the Golden Circle Treasures; Vasquez's Bandit Loot; Lost Arch Mine; Black Beard's Treasure; etc.

As an expert with all kinds of metal detectors and he won numerous National Metal Detecting Contests. His collection of items found is impressive. He has taught courses on Treasure Hunting, Ghost Towns and Gold Prospecting at UCLA, Los Angeles City College, the Elks Lodge in Glendale, Keene Engineering, the Treasure Emporium, taught Metal Detecting to the FBI, and is the consultant on Metal Detecting to the Los Angeles City Police Department. Currently, He is featured in the popular commercial video "Prospecting for Gold," available at most Gold Prospecting and Treasure Hunting shops.

He is a popular guest speaker on these subjects to many clubs and organizations, including "The Gene Autry Museum of Western History;" "The Gold Prospectors Association," "The Adventures' Club of Los Angeles," and has himself been the subject of many newspaper and magazine articles, television and radio programs. He has served as technical consultant for numerous treasure publications and television programs--plus featured in some including "Unsolved Mysteries," "The Treasure Hunters," "The Search for Amazing Treasures," Bill Burrud's "Treasure Series," NBC's specials on "Gold Prospecting" and "Treasure Hunting."

He owns one of the largest private libraries on Treasure Hunting in the world that includes thousands of books, magazine and newspaper articles, videos, tapes and photographs.

www.ingramcontent.com/pod-product-compliance
Lightning Source LLC
Chambersburg PA
CBHW060317240426
43661CB00059B/2793